Cosmo B. Henderson:

What ARE You Doing?

Written by Joanna Nadin

Illustrated by Ned Woodman

Pearson Australia
(a division of Pearson Australia Group Pty Ltd)
707 Collins Street, Melbourne, Victoria 3008
PO Box 23360, Melbourne, Victoria 8012
www.pearson.com.au

Story by Joanna Nadin
Illustrated by Ned Woodman
Designed by Bigtop
First published 2011 by Pearson Education Limited
This edition published 2012 by Pearson Australia
2019 2018 2017 2016
10 9 8 7 6 5 4 3 2

ISBN 978 1 4425 5763 5

Pearson Australia Group Pty Ltd
ABN 40 004 245 943

Acknowledgements
We would like to thank the following for permission to reproduce copyright material.
Cover background © Photocell/Shutterstock; cover notebook image © Klikk/iStockphoto
Every effort has been made to trace and acknowledge copyright. However, if any infringement has occurred, the publishers tender their apologies and invite the copyright holders to contact them.
Printed in Australia by the SOS Print + Media Group

FRIDAY 3RD DECEMBER

WHAT I WANT FOR CHRISTMAS

by Cosmo B. Henderson

1. A new name. I mean, what's wrong with Tom or Jack? It wouldn't matter so much if the "B" stood for Billy or Bob or Ben. But no, my middle name is "Brilliant" and I am NOT EVEN JOKING.

2. My little sister Dido to start wearing a uniform instead of random costumes because there is NOTHING COOL about being followed around by an egg carton crocodile every recess.

3. Kirk Perry to have
a brain transplant.
Because the one he
has at the moment
keeps telling him
to tie me to the
drainpipe outside the
school office. Which
FUNNILY ENOUGH I
do not enjoy.

4. Misty Meadows to be able to keep secrets. Because it's bad enough that my best friend is a GIRL and FREAKISHLY tall, but she cannot help telling EVERYONE EVERYTHING.

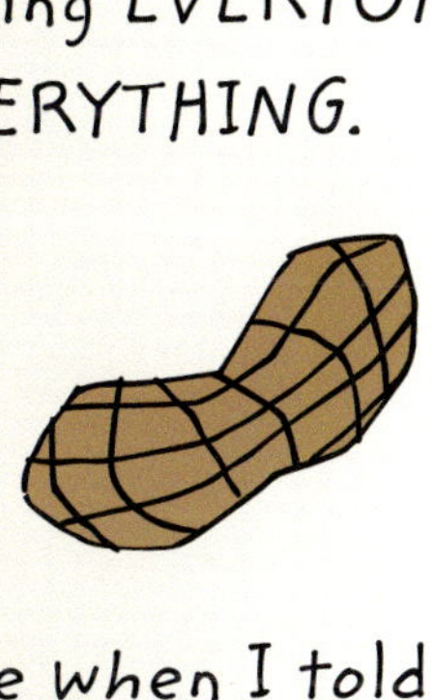

Like when I told her I once got a peanut stuck up my nose and had to go to hospital to get it out, and by recess the whole school was calling me "peanut brain".

5. Lucinda Atkins to notice me in a GOOD way. Because at the moment she mostly says stuff like, "Cosmo B. Henderson, you are such an UTTER WEIRDO." And it wouldn't matter so much if I didn't notice good stuff about her. But the thing is, I sort of do. Misty says it is chemistry and there is nothing I can do about it. She read it in a magazine. I think I like Lucinda's hair, which is really long and swishy.

Obviously, I didn't hand this list in to Miss Singh-Jones. I wrote another one with stuff like "world peace" and "a games console" on it, like everyone else (even though there's no way Mum would ever get me a games console because she says computer games melt your brain).

The annoying thing is, Lucinda Atkins is right. I AM an UTTER WEIRDO. Mum says it's important to stand out in life, but I think it would be better if we ALL faded into the background, so that I could get through Year 6 without being the class FREAK. But I'm pretty sure there is NO chance of that EVER happening.

It's like Misty says: "Cosmo B. Henderson, YOUR LIFE STINKS."

SATURDAY 4TH DECEMBER

I have thought of another thing to add to my list:

6. A new dog, because our dog, Paxman, is just EMBARRASSING. For a start, he is a Labradoodle (which sounds made up, and probably should be, but totally ISN'T). On top of that he has dyed ginger hair, because Mum decided to henna him when she did her own hair, and so now he is like this curly orange clown wig on legs.

AND as if that wasn't enough, he EATS ANYTHING. Seriously.

So far this morning, he has eaten an orange, a fork and a gas bill. Mum says at least the last one shows some sense but she is wrong. I mean, I bet Kirk Perry's dog, Killer, doesn't eat gas bills. Only mortal enemies. Like me.

SUNDAY 5TH DECEMBER

And another thing:

7. A haircut. Because right now, it is too long and full of NITS because Mum does not like to use chemicals (yet she is happy to henna Paxman) and just covered my hair in mayonnaise instead, because her friend Crazy Stella told her it was just as good. So I had to spend an entire day being called "egg head" by Kirk Perry and having to sit at the back of the class because of the smell.

Plus, FUNNILY ENOUGH, it DID NOT WORK, which is unsurprising given that it was CRAZY Stella's idea (I mean, the clue is in the name), so now my head is like something from a horror film.

Oh, and Mum says she CANNOT cut my hair because she has had a scissor phobia ever since she accidentally snipped a bit off her brother's toe when she was seven. SERIOUSLY. So I will have to wait until she can book me in with Julie from next door who works at Curl Up And Dye.

MONDAY 6TH DECEMBER

Our class is going totally MAD with excitement because Miss Singh-Jones says we are allowed an end-of-term disco after all, because Mr Grimes, the caretaker, has fixed the pipes that broke when Kirk Perry tried to recreate a tidal wave inside the school hall.

Misty says a disco is an excellent opportunity to try out her chemistry theory with me and Lucinda Atkins because I can ask her to dance. She says that if there is electricity I will know for sure that she is THE ONE, and it is not just the swishiness of her hair that is mesmerising me.

Only I said that it is all very well testing out scientific theories but I am not sure that Lucinda Atkins will agree: (a) if I am wearing anything out of my wardrobe because, apart from my skinny jeans, most of it is multicoloured from the day Misty and I decided to tie-dye everything, and anyway, my skinny jeans have gone mysteriously missing, possibly inside Paxman. And: (b) unless I get a haircut, but Julie from next door says she will not do it if I am infested again. So Mum says it will have to be Deedee Dent at Loose Ends because she is short-sighted and will not see the nits. Only I pointed out that this means she also would not see my hair to cut it properly, so I am in a total NO WIN situation.

TUESDAY 7TH DECEMBER

It was Misty's idea – the haircut I mean.

During our Science lesson we had to cut up bits of cardboard to make into a model of an oil rig, only Miss Singh-Jones had to take Kirk Perry to see Mr Phelps, our principal, because he threatened to cut Lyndon Jones' leg off. And Misty said she knew how to do haircuts because she'd read about it in a magazine, and then she just snipped off a bit at the back and said, "See?"

Then I had this MASSIVE gap at the back, so I had to let her do the rest otherwise I would have looked WEIRD.

Only now I think I might look even MORE weird because there is only one centimetre left and in some places NO HAIR AT ALL. I mean, at least Kirk Perry's is even, except where he has the arrow shaved into it.

Miss Singh-Jones was not happy at all and sent both of us to Mr Phelps, who was also not happy, but that is probably because he was worried that my mum would blame him and threaten to have a sit-in at school until he couldn't take any more, which is EXACTLY what she did when Dido got sent home by our last principal, Mr Crab, for wearing a balaclava. Mum said she was being a letterbox, but Mr Crab said it broke school rules on identity and in the end Mum had a sit-in and now Mr Crab has retired early and lives in Cairns. Luckily Mum said she was totally on our side because it is our HUMAN RIGHT to cut our own hair whenever we want, even in Science.

Anyway, like I told Mum, at least the nits have gone. Although I don't think Lucinda Atkins likes my new haircut. She said, "Cosmo B. Henderson, you look like a criminal."

WEDNESDAY 8TH DECEMBER

Sometimes I wish Mr Crab was still our principal because Mr Phelps is full of BAD ideas. Like now he has decided to have a Mum/Dad/Carer TALENT competition right before the end-of-term disco to raise money for rescued battery chickens. Lucinda Atkins is totally excited about it because her stepdad is a famous actor in a TV show (he is a doctor who is secretly in love with a nurse, only she is an undercover police officer investigating him for murder), and her mum was once in an ad for shampoo, so she says they are DEFINITELY going to win.

I am NOT EVEN telling Mum about it. If she finds out, my life will be over. Or at least my life for the next year until I go to Harold Wilson High, where no one will know about me or about the time Mum made me wear her underwear to school because the washing machine was broken.

Plus, there is no way Lucinda Atkins is going to test Misty's chemistry theory with me at the school disco if she has just seen Mum doing one of her crazy dances on stage. I mean, what if she thinks that I am going to do weird mime movements too?

Oh, and it is totally a GOOD THING that I have no hair because Dido is scratching again and so is Paxman, and Mum has gone to buy another jar of mayonnaise.

THURSDAY 9TH DECEMBER

The whole class has gone talent show mad. Lucinda Atkins' mum and stepdad are doing a medley of show tunes, Kirk Perry's dad is going to do a dog show with Killer and even Misty's mum is going to tap dance to "New York, New York". I asked Misty if she was going to be embarrassed, but she said only if her mum hits her head on the ceiling, which is totally possible as her mum is also freakishly tall.

Miss Singh-Jones asked what my mum was doing for the show, and I said she isn't allowed to sing or dance because she has purple fever. Which is a total lie, but I really think this is one of those times when lying is okay. Like if your mum says, "Do you like my new dress?" and you say, "YES," even though it looks like a parachute. You are just protecting her. And that is what I was doing. I was protecting Mum and me from a lifetime of SHAME, although she seems to welcome shame. Otherwise why would she bring a mayonnaise-covered, ginger-dyed clown dog to pick me up from school?

And I would have gotten away with it too, except that then Lucinda Atkins put up her hand and said, "Miss Singh-Jones, Cosmo B. Henderson is lying because purple fever is not even REAL and I should know because my stepdad is a DOCTOR." So I said he isn't an ACTUAL doctor, he is an ACTOR doctor. Which even Miss Singh-Jones agreed with. But I was the one who was sent to Mr Phelps because Miss Singh-Jones looked on the internet and realised purple fever is totally made up.

FRIDAY 10TH DECEMBER

Today I have eaten a sheet of A4 paper. I am NOT EVEN JOKING.

It is because Mr Phelps (who is totally obsessed with EMBARRASSING us all) put a letter in everyone's book bags reminding parents that they need to sign up for the talent show by Monday. Which was okay because I was just going to put mine straight into the class recycling box while Miss Singh-Jones was busy telling Kirk Perry off for trying to pencil-sharpen Lyndon Jones' finger, only then I remembered I had to pick up Dido.

As soon as Dido saw me she grabbed my book bag and wouldn't give it back. She said it was her fairy purse (she was wearing wings and a tutu) and couldn't let go or she would DIE, which is ridiculous because why would fairies die if you took their purses?

Anyway, she refused until we got home and she decided to dress up as a spaniel, and spaniels don't have purses, so she left it in the bathroom.

So I got out the note and was totally about to flush it down the loo when Dido came back in and made this speech about how flushing the wrong kind of thing down toilets, like paper or toys, was BAD for the environment and also the plumbing (this is because Rory O'Grady, who is in her class, blocked up a toilet with a plastic turtle last week).

So I told her to be quiet, and then she started shouting and saying I was SUPRESSING her RIGHT TO SPEAK.

Then I panicked because I could hear Mum coming up the stairs, and there is no bin in the bathroom because Dido is using it as a snail house, which is how I ended up eating the talent show letter in a bid to destroy the evidence, which was TOTALLY GROSS and TOTALLY WEIRD.

I would have fed it to Paxman, only he was too busy trying to get some mayonnaise out of his ear. Seriously. He eats ANYTHING. Once he ate the TV remote control and every time he barked the channel changed. That got a bit annoying when I was trying to watch a cartoon and Paxman kept switching it to a programme about bees.

WOOF!
WOOF!

in

out

SATURDAY 11TH DECEMBER

I am BORED. This is because normally on a Saturday Misty comes over and we make ice-cream spiders out of everything in the fridge and watch cartoons. Only this morning when she rang I told her I had mumps, which is another lie, but I know if she comes over she won't be able to RESIST telling Mum about the talent show, so it is in a GOOD CAUSE.

Although maybe I do have mumps because I don't feel that well, and I was a bit late with having my vaccinations because when I was five Mum decided she didn't believe in vaccinations. She said it was her HUMAN RIGHT to refuse them, and she was never letting anyone else in the family go near a needle ever since Paxman had a flu jab and then ate an egg timer on the same day.

Which is what she told Dr Braithwaite. Only he asked if she'd rather I spend weeks covered in spots with a hacking cough or possibly even DEAD. And Mum had a panic that I was going to die, so the next week she booked me an appointment, only Dr Braithwaite couldn't see me for two months because of the swine flu epidemic.

Anyway, the point is, all I have to do now is keep Misty away from the house until next Friday and everything will be fine and life will be back to normal. Or as normal as it gets when you are called Cosmo, and your sister thinks she's a dog, and your dog thinks it's a rubbish bin.

SUNDAY 12TH DECEMBER

OK, so on the good side, I don't have mumps. It was just the sheet of paper making me feel strange, but it's out now, which I won't go into. Also, I'm not bored anymore. But on the BAD side, MUM KNOWS ABOUT THE SHOW.

This is because Mrs Meadows, i.e. Misty's mum, wanted to go into town to get Misty's Christmas present and needed to do it in PRIVATE (which is pointless as Misty already knows she is getting rollerblades, because her mum is as bad as she is when it comes to keeping secrets). Anyway, she rang Mum and asked if she could mind Misty for a bit, and before I could puff my cheeks out to look mumpish, Mum said YES.

So then Misty arrived and she was okay for a bit because I made her stay in my room and play chess (only there are no chess pieces because Paxman ate most of them so we have to use jelly beans and plastic bricks, which is kind of complicated).

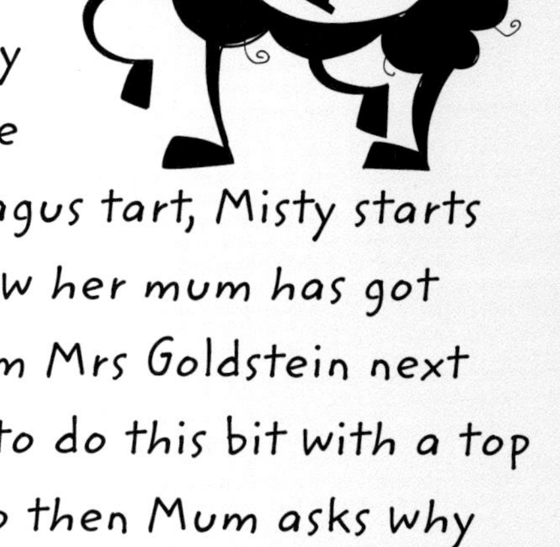

But then Mum said lunch was ready, and halfway through eating the cheese and asparagus tart, Misty starts going on about how her mum has got a gold leotard from Mrs Goldstein next door and is going to do this bit with a top hat and a cane. So then Mum asks why Misty's mum is doing anything with a gold leotard and a top hat etc. and Misty just blabs EVERYTHING.

So now Mum is TOTALLY ANNOYED with me for not telling her before and also TOTALLY EXCITED about the show and is RIGHT NOW thinking up her act with Dido. Which means it will probably

involve dog outfits or singing songs about dead sheep, which is what Dido has been doing all morning.

Misty says at least she lasted two hours, which is a new record. But, like I said, that doesn't make up for the fact that come Friday I AM GOING TO DIE. Or possibly worse, WISH I WAS DEAD.

Misty says I am being NEGATIVE and I should concentrate on positive action, i.e. finding my skinny jeans for the disco. So we did a forensic search of the whole house and found $3.55 in change, a telephone and a stuffed fox, but NOT my skinny jeans.

So then we went through my wardrobe and have narrowed it down to three choices:

1. a pair of shorts and a raincoat
2. a karate kit
3. my school uniform.

Misty says it's not about what you wear, which is true. Only I still don't think Lucinda Atkins is going to want to dance with someone in wet weather gear or karate whites.

MONDAY 13TH DECEMBER

Something has compromised the scientific experiment, i.e. Kirk Perry has asked Lucinda Atkins to the disco. SERIOUSLY. Misty says there is NO WAY she will say yes because his whole family is scary - his nan even went to prison! But I pointed out that his nan only went to prison for a day because she didn't pay her council rates and at least his head is shaved evenly.

Oh, and Mum has put her name on the sign-up sheet for the talent show. Lucinda Atkins came up to me right away and demanded to know what talent my Mum had. I said it was a secret (which it is, because Mum is refusing to tell me so that "it will be a surprise on the night", which is worse, if you ask me) so Lucinda swished her hair and said, "Well, I don't expect SHE went to the Fawcett Academy for Dramatic Arts like my stepdad, or was ever in a shampoo ad." And then, for some reason, I said, "That's what you think. Actually she is pretty amazing, my mum, so you had better watch out." Then Lucinda Atkins got all red in the face and swished her hair so hard it whipped Pippa Ridgeby in the eye, and then she said, "Cosmo B. Henderson, you are SUCH a liar."

Then she stormed off and Pippa Ridgeby had to go to Mr Phelps to sit down for a bit because she couldn't see.

WHY did I say that? WHY? Because: (a) now Lucinda Atkins will definitely say YES to Kirk Perry and NO to my scientific experiment.

And: (b) I am pretty sure that Mum has NO talent whatsoever. I mean, the last time she did acting, she was pretending to be a horse with Dido and it was totally NOT convincing at all. I mean, since when do horses moo?

Misty says I need to look on the positive side. But like I said, I've got just four days to AVERT DISASTER and where is the positive in that?

TUESDAY 14TH DECEMBER

Lucinda Atkins has told Kirk Perry she will NOT go to the disco with him because: (a) he eats bees which is cruel (this is true, I have seen him do it, only it wasn't to be cruel, it was to prove he is immune to pain);

and (b) she likes someone else. Part of me thought that maybe, just maybe, it was me. Only most of me thought that it was probably Lyndon Jones because he has a black belt in karate and a horse. But Misty says this is definitely positive side NUMBER ONE. And positive side NUMBER TWO is that if it was up to Captain Fabulous (who is this superhero in a comic book, who she is totally obsessed with) he wouldn't sit

COSMO
LUCINDA

around feeling totally sorry for himself. He would come up with a plan of action. I said, "I bet Captain Fabulous' mum doesn't try to kill nits with mayonnaise," but Misty said I was being NEGATIVE again and that wouldn't solve anything. Which she is right about. Annoyingly.

So at lunch, when everyone else was swapping football cards or pretending to be pop stars, we wrote our ACTION PLAN TO AVERT DISASTER. It looks like this:

Plan A

Create an emergency so that Mum has to deal with that and CAN'T GO TO THE SHOW.

Plan B

Be sick so that Mum has to look after me and CAN'T GO TO THE SHOW.

Plan C

Sabotage the school so that Mr Phelps has to cancel everything and Mum CAN'T GO TO THE SHOW.

Tomorrow we're going to try Plan A – create an emergency. We are going to help Paxman run away. Well, not really run away, but just go missing for a while. Because if he goes missing, then Mum will HAVE to spend the rest of the week looking for him because she says Paxman is "like a son" to her. Even if he does have curly orange hair and ate a stapler and two lumps of coal this morning. Which, I pointed out, I would never do, but Mum said she would love me even if I ate the kitchen sink. Which I guess is actually pretty good, given that I swallowed a sheet of A4 paper four days ago.

WEDNESDAY 15TH DECEMBER

So Plan A didn't QUITE work out.

It started off okay. Misty and I offered to take Paxman for a walk straight after school. Mum was busy making a beaver helmet with Dido so she said, "That's very kind of you, Cosmo B. Henderson," which made me feel kind of bad, but not bad enough not to do it.

So we walked all the way into town, and Misty was going to let him off the lead in the hardware shop, because there are a lot of weird things he likes to eat in there, but I said we should go to the library because it is on three floors and once I got lost for an hour in the history section.

So then we thought up pros and cons for each place, only by the time we had decided on the library, we realised Paxman had disappeared anyway. We looked in the hardware shop and in the library, but he was TOTALLY missing. And I know that was the point, except then it didn't seem like such a good idea any more because I felt REALLY sick about Paxman being lost and no one helping him, because he looks so weird and mostly people just laugh.

Then Misty went home because she had a tuba lesson, and I walked round the park for a bit shouting, "Paxman, Paxman." Mr Wrigley from Banksia Drive, who was walking his dog, Muffet, (who is brown and a Yorkshire Terrier, i.e.

TOTALLY NORMAL) kept giving me funny looks like he thought I was UP TO NO GOOD. He thinks all children are usually UP TO NO GOOD, although in the case of Kirk Perry he is usually right. So I went home. But UNBELIEVABLY, when I got there, Paxman was ALREADY HOME, sitting on the couch watching the news.

I asked Mum what he was doing there, and she said, "He likes the weather report for some reason." So I said, "Not ON THE COUCH, I mean AT HOME, because I thought he was lost." And Mum said, "Someone called Mrs Potts accidentally sat on him on the bus after her Senior Swim and brought him home!"

And then she said, "But WHAT was he doing on a bus in the first place, Cosmo B. Henderson? That's what I'd like to know." So I said, "Maybe he felt like having an adventure," and Mum agreed that that was the sort of unique thing Paxman might do. To be honest, I felt relieved because even though he is a ginger clown dog who eats furniture, he is kind of funny.

Only now I only have TWO DAYS left to avert disaster. Misty says I am being NEGATIVE again, and tomorrow we can do Plan B. Which she's right about.

And she's right about something else as well. Captain Fabulous wouldn't have forgotten to take the address tag off Paxman's collar.

THURSDAY 16TH DECEMBER

We got the idea in History. It was because we were learning all about the Black Death, and Miss Singh-Jones asked us if there were any modern plagues we could think of and Lucinda Atkins, who is always first to answer questions, stuck her hand up and said, "Me, Miss, me," and Miss Singh-Jones looked to see if anyone else wanted to answer but no one did. So she sighed and said, "Yes, Lucinda?" and Lucinda said, "Swine flu, Miss. I know that because my stepdad is a doctor." Miss Singh-Jones said, "That is right, Lucinda." Which meant that she got a gold star (even though her stepdad is NOT an ACTUAL doctor and even though she already has forty-eight. I've only got twenty-three, but at least it's better than Kirk Perry who has eight. He did have nine but one got taken away

when he squeezed his head between the railings and got it stuck and they had to call the fire brigade to saw him out).

Anyway, the point is that I am going to have FAKE swine flu tomorrow morning so that Mum has to look after me and can't do the show. Then I am going to get miraculously better in time for the disco and Lucinda Atkins will be so relieved that I am alive she will definitely dance with me. Misty says it is GENIUS and NOTHING can go wrong. She had better be right, otherwise I am going to wish I had REAL Black Death, rather than FAKE swine flu.

FRIDAY 17TH DECEMBER

Something WEIRD has happened. And NOT in the normal sense of WEIRD. But in the weird sense of NORMAL. Which probably won't make sense until you read this:

So to start with, Plan B went TOTALLY to plan.

I thought
at one point
I had overdone it
with the purple spots
on my face
(one of Dido's felt tips),
because I'm not too sure
exactly
what the symptoms
of swine flu are.

But Mum waved her hands over my head and said my aura was definitely damaged and that I had to lie down IMMEDIATELY and drink lavender tea, which is gross and tastes like soap, but BELIEVE ME, it is better than watching Mum embarrass herself (and me) in front of the WHOLE SCHOOL, and especially Lucinda Atkins.

Then Mum got Julie from next door to take Dido to school, and I could tell Julie wasn't too pleased because Dido was wearing a spacesuit, but she did it anyway because she has to go that way to her job at Curl Up And Dye. So then I got to spend the WHOLE morning on the couch watching cartoons while Mum rang Crazy Stella to find out other remedies for swine flu that wouldn't involve REAL medicine. Which for once I was relieved about because I'm pretty sure Dr Braithwaite would not be fooled by the felt tips.

After lunch, Mum said she had an exciting surprise for me, which for one minute I thought actually MIGHT be a games console, because Kirk Perry got one when he had the flu, although his mum said it was to shut him up because the whining "did her head in".

But UNSURPRISINGLY the surprise was a lot less exciting. It was CRAZY STELLA. Mum said she had offered to look after me for the afternoon. And that meant Mum could go and be in the talent show. I swear I was ALMOST ACTUALLY SICK and

I would have begged Mum to change her mind but she had already whizzed off to school to RUIN MY LIFE and I was left alone with Crazy Stella.

So NOT ONLY was Mum about to SHAME me without me even getting to see it, but I also had to spend several hours with a woman who has a bigger moustache than Mr Crab, and who actually believes in pixies. SERIOUSLY.

I decided I needed to get out of there fast and do Plan C, i.e. sabotage the school, i.e. set off the fire alarms, like Kirk Perry did once in assembly and we all had to stand outside in the rain even though it was OBVIOUS there was no fire because WHERE WAS THE SMOKE?

So I let Stella do a magic chant over me, and then said, "Wow, Stella, I feel amazingly better. In fact, SO much better that I think I could go back to school." And Stella was so pleased that she said, "Great, because I am DYING to see Cherry (i.e. my mum) do her THING." I said, "What is her THING exactly?" But Crazy Stella said,

Which made me feel sick all over again. But I didn't have time to worry about that, or the fact that I was about to arrive at school with a woman with a moustache, and a ginger curly clown dog, because I had a show to stop.

When I got to school the hall was PACKED and I could see the fire alarm behind Miss Singh-Jones, but between me and her were about a hundred people including Kirk Perry and Lucinda Atkins. So I started pushing through them all, and I didn't stop.

Not when Lucinda screamed and said,

"Oh my gosh, it's Cosmo B. Henderson, and he's contagious!"

Not when Kirk Perry tripped me so that I ended up in Pippa Ridgeby's lap.

Not when Miss Singh-Jones said,

"That is four gold stars I am knocking off your tally, young man."

I didn't stop until my finger was touching the fire alarm bell.

But that's when the WEIRD thing happened, because then the whole room went quiet and I heard Mum's voice. And AMAZINGLY it wasn't shouting, "Cosmo B. Henderson, WHAT do you think you are doing?" It was singing. And it was BEAUTIFUL.

I am NOT EVEN JOKING. Mum CAN SING! And not the usual humming she does in the kitchen when she is making dinner. This was proper opera stuff, with warbling bits and everything. In fact, she can sing so well that she made Miss Singh-Jones cry.

Plus she totally beat Mr and Mrs Atkins, whose show medley fell apart when Paxman tried to join in, AND Kirk Perry's dad and Killer, who got disqualified for trying to bribe the judges, and EVEN Misty's mum, who didn't hit her head, but did accidentally poke Mr Phelps in the ear with her cane.

But Misty doesn't mind, because, as she says, "Cosmo B. Henderson, your life ISN'T so stinky anymore."

And you know what, I think she's right. Even though Paxman ate a microphone and Lyndon Jones' trainers.

Even though Crazy Stella had to be taken to Mr Phelps' office for trying to summon up goblins from under the climbing frame. And EVEN THOUGH it wasn't until I was up on stage that I realised I was STILL WEARING MY PYJAMAS. Which I figured was so NOT the kind of outfit that would make Lucinda Atkins want to do the scientific experiment.

Only the thing is – she DID. She actually DANCED with me, once I'd shown her that my spots were felt tip and that I wasn't contagious. And even though it was only one dance, and even though straight after she went off with Lyndon Jones because he promised she could ride his horse tomorrow, and even though I am pretty sure there were no actual sparks or anything, which is what Misty said there would be, I think maybe she doesn't hate me. She might even like me. Just a little bit.

So I think I might want world peace for Christmas after all.

COSMO

LUCINDA